W0115550

Children's Sermons
—— Year C ——

Rev. Dr. Lal Hmingliani Browne

Illustrated by

Elizabeth Browne & Emily Browne

© Rev. Dr. Lal Hmingliani Browne.

All rights reserved. This book or any portion thereof may not be reproduced or used in any manner whatsoever without the express written permission of the publisher except for the use of brief quotations in a book review.

ISBN: 978-1-09839-983-2 (printed)

ISBN: 978-1-09839-984-9 (eBook)

DEDICATION

To my parents, who took us,

their 6 children,

seriously enough to tell us Bible stories most every night.

These stories shaped us

into faithful and joyful disciples of Christ.

With deep gratitude, I also dedicate this book

to all the children

whom I have ever told Bible stories

during children's sermons in worship.

FORWARD

Children's Sermons Year C

Most every day of my growing-up years, my father told us Bible stories. I really loved that.

I always enjoy reading Children's Sermon books. Inspired by them, I have always wanted to write such a book.

In doing Children's Sermons, while I think I am teaching the children, they are teaching me and I am learning a great deal about God' faithfulness and love from them.

I believe that:

- Children are participants not an audience;

- Children have insights that are valuable faith lessons for all of us to learn;

- Children take God and Jesus seriously and with faith;

- My hope is to share the stories of the Bible – particularly stories about Jesus – in a way that children are engaged and encouraged to think of how they apply to their lives;

- Children are brilliant in learning that the Gospel is for all people in all places, of every condition, speaking any language, with any physical characteristics

This book is aimed to engage Bible stories with children. I hope this book is somewhat useful to you in your ministry with the children. Feel free to use it however it fits your context of ministry.

It has been great fun to write with my granddaughters, Elizabeth age 13 and Emily age 9, providing the illustrations and with my husband, Rev. Dr. Will Browne, providing editing help. All of the scriptures quoted are from the NRSV.

*I have chosen to follow the lectionary as found in the Presbyterian Church (USA). However, all of the scriptures chosen for comment are also in the lectionary as found in the Vanderbilt listing.

In God's Grace and Peace,

Hmingi

On sabbatical summer 2021

First Sunday of Advent- November 28, 2021

Luke 21:29-33 "HOPE"

Color – Purple

Resources: An Advent wreath of greens with 3 purple candles, 1 pink candle and 1 white candle in the middle of the wreath. A banner that says "HOPE."

Children's Sermon: Look around and tell me what do you see in the Church that was not here last Sunday. *Let the children answer you.*

Yes, there are Christmas-looking decorations here in the church, because today is the first Sunday of Advent. Look over here, I brought an Advent wreath for you to see. We begin advent season today. It is from today until Christmas eve. The color in Church in this season is purple because purple is a color for royalty and Jesus is our royalty.

Today we light one of the purple candles. It is called the candle of HOPE as Jesus is our hope. Jesus is the hope for the whole world.

We begin preparing for the arrival of baby Jesus today. When I was growing up, my dad would lead the whole family in cleaning and decorating our house on a day like today. We would use colorful streamers and a big paper star with a light bulb in it for the top of our front door. It was so much fun. If your house is not decorated yet, please ask you parents to decorate and prepare your houses and your hearts to welcome Jesus who will arrive on Christmas day. And, I almost forgot to tell you that the greens around the wreath mean God's love for us is a never-ending love.

The scripture today tells us that there are signs and seasons in our lives and Church. Today we begin the season of Advent. We begin preparing and waiting for baby Jesus to arrive. Let us pray. Repeat after me.

Prayer:

Dear God, thank you for loving us all the time. Thank you for this season of Advent we just started. Help us to be patient as we prepare ourselves for the arrival of baby Jesus. In his name we pray. Amen.

Hope   Peace

Second Sunday of Advent - December 5, 2021

Luke 3:1-6 "Peace"
Color – Purple

Resources: An Advent wreath of greens with 3 purple candles, 1 pink candle and one white candle in the middle of the wreath. Also, a banner that says "PEACE."

Children's Sermon: Today is the second Sunday of Advent. We are still preparing for Jesus' arrival. How is it going in your houses? Any decorations yet? *Let the Children answer you.*

How is it in your hearts? Have you told God that you love God and that you are getting ready for baby Jesus? *Let the children answer you.*

Today is the Second Sunday of Advent and we light the second purple candle. It is also called the candle of Peace. This reminds us that Jesus is our Prince of Peace and we celebrate the Peace we get from Jesus today. In the scripture lesson today, we see that John-the-Baptist prepared the way for Jesus - just like we are doing here now. Let us pray. Repeat after me please.

Prayer:
Dear God, we thank you for loving us all the time. Thank you for Jesus our Prince of Peace. Please teach us how to live peacefully with everyone around us. In Jesus name we pray. Amen.

3

Third Sunday of Advent - December 12, 2021
Luke 3:10-18 "Love"
Color – Pink

Resources: An Advent wreath of greens with 3 purple candles, 1 pink candle and one white candle in the middle. Also, a banner that says "LOVE."

Children's Sermon: Today we light the pink candle. It is called the Candle of Love. It represents God's love for us. Today we are all about love.

During this time of the year in my culture (both Mizo and Myanmar) we get together with families and friends and even strangers who are interested. We have big feasts with lots of food. We eat, we talk, we laugh and we sing lots of Christmas carols. That's how we prepare ourselves and get ready for Christmas. It is a lot of fun. Children sing along and play too.
Do you do things like that? *Let the children answer you.*

In our scripture lesson today – Jesus tells us to share food with others. He also tells us that we should share our clothing with those who are poor and are in need of it. In these cold winter months especially, it would be good to donate your warm clothes that you don't wear anymore to those who can use them. Let us pray. Please repeat after me.

Prayer:
Dear God, thank you for loving us all the time. Thank you for Jesus who taught us to share our blessings from you. Help us prepare for Jesus' arrival with generosity and love. In his name we pray. Amen.

Fourth Sunday of Advent - December 19, 2021
Luke 1:39-40 "Joy"
Color – Purple

Resources: An Advent wreath of greens with 3 purple candles, 1 pink candle and one white candle in the middle. Also, a banner that says "JOY."

Children's Sermon: It is almost Christmas friends! Today we light a purple candle called the Candle of Joy. We are all about joy as our wait for the baby Jesus is almost over. The Bible tells us about Mary, Jesus' mommy, who was pregnant, meeting her cousin Elizabeth who was also pregnant with John the Baptist.

Do you remember seeing a pregnant lady? *Let the children answer you.*

I remember my mom being pregnant 4 times. She gave birth to my 3 sisters and twin brothers. I got to be the oldest of 6 children. I really like that. Where I grew up, families were big like that. Now they just have 2 or 3 children in a family there.

Back to our Bible story today. When Mary and Elizabeth met, the unborn baby, John, made a lot of happy movements in his mommy's womb. He was feeling Jesus' presence in his mommy's womb. John was so joyful.

Let us be full of happiness and joy as the day of Christmas is almost here. Let's keep getting ready for baby Jesus to arrive. Exciting! Isn't it? Let us pray. Please repeat after me.

Prayer
Dear God, thank you for loving us all the time. Christmas is almost here and please help us to prepare ourselves with love and joy because you love us so. In Jesus' name. Amen.

Christmas Eve - December 24, 2021
Luke 2:1-14 "The birth of Jesus"
Color – White

Resources: A creche without the three wise men.

Children's Sermon: Today we light the white candle which is also called the Christ Candle. Because we are not going to be worshipping in the Church tomorrow, we are having a Christmas service this evening. We celebrate baby Jesus being born.

The Bible tells us that Jesus' mom and dad, Mary and Joseph, went to register themselves in the town called Bethlehem in Judea. Mary had to give birth and there was no room in the inn. So, they ended up in a stable. Mary gave birth to baby Jesus and they wrapped him in cloth and put him in a manger. The angels came to sing, "Glory to God in the highest heaven, Peace on earth!" for baby Jesus. The shepherds also came from far away. They were all so happy and joyful.

Are we also happy and joyful that baby Jesus is born? *Let the children answer you.*

Our wait and preparing is over. Please repeat after me, "Glory to God in the highest heaven, peace on earth!"

Have a lot of fun tomorrow on Christmas day celebrating Jesus birth with your family, friends and God's love!!! Let us pray. Please repeat after me.

Prayer:
Dear God, thank you for loving us all the time. We thank you that our wait for baby Jesus is over and he is here! We love you God for sending Jesus to us. May this Christmas be a joyful one for everyone. In Jesus name. Amen.

Happy Christmas!

Happy Christmas!

Happy Christmas!

Christmas Chibai!

(In Mizo)

First Sunday of Christmas

December 26   Christmas Celebrations

Luke 2:41-52

Color - White

Resources: Christmas paper wrapped boxes of different sizes. Or Christmas bags.

Children's Sermon: Merry Christmas Children! Where I grew up we say, "Happy Christmas!"

Jesus is born and we are here celebrating now. Please tell me what happened in your house yesterday morning besides eating a delicious breakfast? *Let the children answer you.*

Yes, of course, opening Christmas presents on Christmas day morning is such fun and a wonderful experience and feelings too. I am glad you all had a good Christmas morning. The best and biggest present to all of us, I mean for all the people in the whole wide world, is baby Jesus. Jesus is God's Present to us to tell us, "I Love You All!" As the days go on in the Christmas Season, would you please remember that Christmas means, "God loves you, me and everyone." Let us pray. Please repeat after me.

Prayer:

Dear God, thank you for loving us all the time. Thank you for your best gift on Christmas day - baby Jesus - who is born to be your love with us. We love you God, with our whole heart today. In Jesus' name. Amen.

Second Sunday of Christmas/Epiphany Sunday - January 2, 2022
Matthew 2:1-12 "The three wise people and gifts"
Color – White

Resources: A creche including 3 wise men. White paper stars. A treasure chest.

Children's Sermon: Please look at this creche. Do you see anything different from Christmas Eve? *Let the children answer you.*

Yes, you are right, we see 3 wise men and their gifts that were not there before. Today is called "Epiphany Sunday." The scripture tells us that the wise men saw a bright star in the sky and knew that baby Jesus was born. So, they packed their treasures of Gold, Frankincense and Myrrh and followed the star all the way to the baby Jesus. When they arrived, they saw baby Jesus, they knelt down before him and gave him their treasure.

Would you please remember that we too can give a gift of treasure to Jesus. We can give him our love from our hearts. That is our treasure for now. Love Jesus just like you love your mom and dad or even more. Let us pray. Please repeat after me.

Prayer:
Dear God, thank you for loving us all the time. Please teach us how to love you back. In Jesus name. Amen.

Baptism of the Lord Sunday - January 9, 2022
Luke 3:15-17; 21-22   "Jesus was Baptized"
Color – White

Resources: An empty bowl. A bottle of water. Or take the children to the Baptismal Font.

Children's Sermon: Today is all about Baptism. Precisely the baptism of Jesus.

Do you remember your own baptism? *Let the children answer you.*

I don't remember mine. I was 9 months old when I got baptized. People can be baptized at any age. I do remember when my younger sister. Seni, was baptized. We lived in the country called Myanmar on a military base – 2 hours bus ride from the city. There was no pastor nearby. So, we had to wait until a pastor from the city could come. And all Christians helped one another there. A Methodist pastor came to baptize my sister in worship.

I know there are many Churches and pastors in every city and towns in this country. Your parents get to choose when they want you to be baptized and where. That was not true where I grew up when I was growing up.

In God's eyes we are all the same. Presbyterians or Methodists or Baptists or Catholic or anything else. God loves us all. In baptism, God claims us as God's own and we become a member of God's family. Jesus was baptized too, because he was fully a human like us.

Let us pray:
Dear God, thank you for loving us all the time. Thank you for welcoming us into your family in baptism. Help us to grow, loving you more every day. In Jesus name we pray. Amen.

Second Sunday after Epiphany Sunday - January 16, 2022
John 2:1-11 "The first miracle of Jesus: Jesus Turned Water into Wine"

Color – Green

Resources: A see-through pitcher of water and a see-through pitcher of grape juice.

Children's Sermon: What is your favorite wine?

Let the children answer you. They may giggle or look lost on their faces or say "I don't know…"

Wine is very important to my people all through our history. They make wine from rice, grapes, bananas, guavas or berries. Most anything really. They make wine step by step, waiting for days for it to become wine. It takes 4 months to 2 years to make good wine from grapes. Grown-ups take wine to celebrate and to give sympathy and just to have a good dinner with friends.

In today's Bible reading, Jesus turned water into wine just like that in no time. He turned water into wine because he had the power and he was helping the wedding people. They ran out of wine and it was getting to be embarrassing. When they were out of wine, Jesus' mother Mary told Jesus, "They have no wine." And she told the stewards to do whatever Jesus told them to do. There were 6 stone jars there and Jesus told the stewards to fill them with water. They filled them up to the brim. Jesus said to them, "Now draw some out and take it to the chief steward." So, they took it to the steward. When the steward tasted it, it was very good wine. Jesus had done a miracle and turned the water into wine. So, everyone was served that good wine and was happy.

There are a few important points here:

- Jesus went to a wedding with his mom - Mary. So nice. If your mom invites you to go somewhere with her, I hope you will go and enjoy being with her.

- Jesus listened to his mother when she said, "They have no more wine." He loved and respected his mother and helped her out. So, we too should love and respect our moms and be helpful at home.

- This was the first time ever that Jesus worked a miracle. It was to help his mom out. How wonderful was that? This story also tells us that even his mother, Mary, trusted Jesus and had faith in him. So should we.

- Mary brought her worry to Jesus. We are invited to do the same because Jesus is near us always. We should pray to Jesus about all our worries. We are also invited to thank him. Let us pray. Please repeat after me.

Prayer:
Dear God, thank you for loving us all the time. Thank you for Jesus and his mother Mary and the story we heard today. Please teach us how to trust you always like Mary did. In Jesus' name we pray. Amen.

17

Third Sunday after Epiphany - January 23, 2022
Luke 4:14-21 "Jesus went to the Synagogue on a Sabbath day in Nazareth"
Color – Green

Resources: A big red paper heart.

Children's Sermon: Jesus went to the synagogue or church on a Sabbath (Sunday for us now) as it was his custom. He went to church and read about the good news of the Bible.

What is a custom? *Let the children answer you.*
A custom is something we do regularly. Jesus went to the church regularly. So do we. We come to learn about:

- God's love for us is forever and ever

- God forgives us if we ask and pray for it

- God who wants us to love one another - that means all kinds of people regardless of skin color, languages, cultures, sexual orientation, poor, rich, physically challenged or not.

We come to:

- sing God's praises

- listen to the scriptures read and sermon preached

- have fellowship with others.

Jesus read the scripture in the church. If you are old enough to read, I would like you to read the scripture/Bible every day. I love to read the Psalms myself. If you are not old enough to read, just listen to the pastor's reading of the Bible. It is good to have a custom or habit of reading the Bible. It is full of the stories of God and God's people.
Jesus went to church regularly and we are invited to do the same. Let us pray. Please repeat after me.

Prayer:
Dear God, thank you for loving us all the time. Teach us to love you and love one another and to love our neighbors. In Jesus name we pray. Amen.

Fourth Sunday after Epiphany - January 30, 2022

I Corinthians 13:1-13 "Love "
Color - Green

Resource: a picture

Children's Sermon: Do you know what love is? Who do you love? *Let the children answer you.*

The Apostle Paul wrote a love poem to the people of Corinth many years ago. He told them that love is patient, kind, not jealous or boastful, arrogant or rude.

Those words are also true for us today. If you love someone, you don't insist on your own way but you tell the truth. You love them and forgive them and accept them. Most of all you accept them and love them. God's love for us never ends. It is always there.

So, would you please remember to forgive and accept those you love? Remember that God loves them as much as God loves you. Let us pray. Please repeat after me.

Prayer:
Dear God, thank you for loving us all the time. Please teach us how to love one another and our neighbor. Most of all, please teach us how to love you back. In Jesus name we pray. Amen.

Fifth Sunday after Epiphany - February 6, 2022
Luke 5:1-11 "Jesus calling his first disciples"
Color – Green

Resources: " A picture of some people fishing or your own picture of fishing"

Children's Sermon: Have you ever gone fishing? *Let the children answer you.*

Oh, I love to go fishing. It is one of my favorite hobbies. It is so disappointing when I did not catch any fish. I am disappointed because I go fishing to catch the fish to eat. I love to eat the fish I catch myself best.

In today's Bible lesson, Jesus was standing on the shore of Lake Gennesaret. He saw 2 boats. The crowd was pushing him, so he got into one those two boats. Jesus talked to the people on the shore from the boat. When that was all finished, Simon, the fisherman, told Jesus that he had been up all night fishing and had caught nothing.

I can almost feel how awful Simon must have felt.

Jesus told him and his brother, Andrew, to take the boat to deeper water and put down the fishing net. So, Simon and Andrew did what Jesus said and caught lots and lots of fish – so many fish that their net almost broke. Simon told Jesus that he had not been a very good person. Jesus said, "Follow me and I will make you a fisher of men." Jesus meant that he would let Simon and his brother, Andrew, bring people to believe in God. Simon and his brother followed Jesus. They became the first 2 disciples of the 12 disciples Jesus had. They told God's love to all the people.

I hope if you go fishing, you catch some fish. Most importantly, I hope you follow Jesus by being loving and kind to all people. Let us pray. Please repeat after me.

Prayer:
Dear God, thank you for loving us all the time. Thank you for the Bible story about fishing and the people. Please teach us how to follow you like Simon and his brother, Andrew, did so many years ago. In Jesus' name we pray. Amen.

Sixth Sunday after Epiphany - Feb 13

Luke 6:17-26 "Beatitudes/ Valentine's day"

Color - green

Resource: A heart shape box of candies. A stem of red rose. A valentines' card.

Children's Sermon: A very special day is coming tomorrow. What is it? *Let the children say, 'Valentine's Day'!!!*

Yes, that is right! What is valentine's day all about? Love, of course. Love for people, certain people in your lives. It is very good to give and receive love. It is also good to give and receive flowers or candies or a nice card. But remember your ultimate Valentine is God who loves you always. And me too.

Today in our scripture, Jesus tells us who are the people that are blessed with God's love.

They are:
- the poor,
- the hungry,
- the sad,
- people who are being wronged, and
- people who are neglected and friendless.

Jesus said these are the very people God loves. So, we should love them too. When Valentine's Day comes tomorrow, would you please remember to love the special people in your lives and also all the people God loves.

Prayer:

Dear God, thank you for loving us all the time. Please teach us to know how to love the people you love and help us to love you back. In Jesus name. Amen.

Seventh Sunday after Epiphany - February 20, 2022
Luke 6:27-38 "Love your enemies. Don't Judge others."
Color – Green

Resources: " A Bible"

Children's Sermon: Do you have enemies? Who is an enemy? *Let the children answer you.*

Well… usually people who want bad things to happen to us are our enemies. Remember last Sunday we talked about who God loves. All kinds of people really. Jesus is telling us in today's scripture to love and pray even for those who are not kind to us. They need love, God's love even more. And remember, God loves everyone.

Jesus also said, "Don't judge others because that is God's job." It is very easy to judge others. I remember one time I was waiting at a restaurant waiting for my friends, Kirsten and Erika, to come. They were late and the waitress brought me coffee. She looked very unhappy and she was grumpy. I was kind of mad at her at first. Then finally I said to her, "Are you ok? I am very sorry my friends are so late in joining me." She started crying. Then she told me what a terrible horrible awful morning she was having. I told her that I would be praying for her and her family. She sat down across the table for a few minutes and I prayed for her and her family. See, I did not know why she was unhappy and grumpy. My first judgement of her look and behavior was very wrong. It is best not to judge others. Especially because Jesus told us not to.

Prayer: Let us pray. Repeat after me.
Dear God, thank you for loving us all the time. Please teach us how to see the good side of others so that we will not judge them. Teach us to know how to love you back. In Jesus' name. Amen.

Transfiguration of the Lord - Feb 27, 2022
Luke 9:28-36 (37-43) "Transfiguration Sunday"
Color – White

Resources: Very very white fabric (at least 2 yards of it).

Children's Sermon: Jesus went up to the mountain with his friends/disciples Peter, James and John to pray. While Jesus was praying, his face and his clothes became dazzling white. Do you know how white that is? What is the whitest thing you have ever seen? *Let the children answer you.*

Dazzling white is whiter than any of us have ever seen!

Suddenly, Moses and Elijah, who had been in heaven for hundreds of years, were talking to Jesus. Peter said, "Let us build houses for Jesus, Moses and Elijah." Then God's voice came in the cloud saying, "This is my son, my beloved, listen to him." And then Elijah and Moses were gone. Peter, James and John were left alone with Jesus again.

You and I are very lucky that the Bible is full of the teachings and stories of Jesus for us. God said "Listen to Jesus." So, we do. How do we listen to Jesus? *Let the children answer you.*

Right. We listen to Jesus by loving God, loving family, friends and neighbors.

Prayer: Let us pray. Please repeat after me.
Dear God, thank you for loving us all the time. Thank you for the teachings and stories of Jesus in the Bible that we can read any time. Thank you for our Sunday school teachers, parents and all those who tell us about Jesus. In Jesus name we pray. Amen.

First Sunday in Lent

March 6, 2022

Luke 4:1-13 "40 days and 40 nights"

Color: Purple

Resource: a picture of Jesus praying

Children's Sermon: Today is the first Sunday in Lent. What is Lent? *Let the children answer you.*

It is a period of six weeks before Easter. We also call it the Lenten Season. During Lenten season, we remember Jesus praying in the wilderness for 40 days and 40 nights without eating. He was tempted by the devil in the wilderness where he was praying. But he never gave in.

During lent, we look at our lives and we try to be better as a person and as a Christian. We pray and we ask God to help us to learn to be a better person.

The color of the Lenten Season, as you see in the Church, is purple. Purple is a royal color and Jesus is our royalty. Remember we use the same color purple during Advent season before Christmas as we were waiting for the baby Jesus to be born.

My friend, Lucinda, told me many years ago that, in the Lenten Season, I should try to do something that is good for someone else in Jesus' name. How about that?

Can you think of something nice you can do for others? *Let the children answer you.*

You can help clean your room, put away your toys without being asked, help with anything your mom or dad might appreciate at home. You might also help your neighbor by walking their dog or something like that. Let us pray, repeat after me.

Prayer:

Dear God, thank you for loving us all the time. Please teach us to pray and to reflect on our lives during the next 40 days. Help us to be more like Jesus every day. We love you. In Jesus name. Amen.

Second Sunday in Lent

March 13, 2022 God is our light and salvation

Psalm 27
Color - Purple

Resource: a picture of light in the darkness

Children's Sermon: Today is the second Sunday in Lent. Did you all do anything extra good for others since last Sunday? *Let the children answer.*

The Psalm for today tells us that God is our light and our salvation and that we should not ever be afraid. God is always with us, loving us, protecting us, teaching us and forgiving us. We are invited to talk to God about anything, anytime in prayer. God is always listening to us and is always ready to answer our prayers.

Prayer: Let us pray. Please repeat after me.
Dear God, thank you for loving us all the time. Thank you for being with us at all times. Please teach us to talk to you in prayers. In Jesus name. Amen.

^^^^^^^**W I N G S**^^^^^^^

SINGING   **SINGING**

Third Sunday in Lent
March 20, 2022

Luke 13:1-9 Singing under God's wings
Color Purple

Resources: a picture of a bird and people under its wings

Children's Sermon: Can you imagine God being a big beautiful bird with huge wings and you are sitting under God's wings singing happily? *Let the children answer you.*

That is the sort of life we have as God's children. God covers us under God's strong, powerful and loving wings because God really loves us. And all the time too.

When I was a kid growing up, I loved to pray or talk to God at night from my bed with my arms and legs all spread apart. That's how I said my nighttime prayers. How do you pray? *Let the children answer you.*

God listens to all our prayers whether we are sitting or lying down or standing up or running or walking. God is always holding us up with love.

Prayer: Let us pray. Please repeat after me.
Dear God, thank you for loving us all the time. Thank you for holding us up and covering us with your strong and beautiful wings. Teach us to be kind to one another. In Jesus name we pray. Amen.

LOVE

FORGIVE

WELCOME

Fourth Sunday in Lent
March 27, 2022

Luke 15:1-3, 11b-32   Prodigal Son story
Color Purple

Resource:

A long long time ago there was a very rich man who has 2 sons. The older one was a real good son with excellent behavior and he worked hard. The younger son was not so good. He asked for his share of his father's money. The father gave it to him. He took the money and spent it all. He became so poor and hungry to a point that he had to eat pig food. One day he decided to go home to his father to ask for forgiveness and ask to be employed as a servant. His father saw him coming to the house. He was so happy to see his younger son again. He ran out of the house and hugged him and gave him a ring and good clothes. The son asked for forgiveness and the father forgave him right away.

Have you ever forgiven someone? *Let the children answer you.*

God is like that for us. If we mess up and make a big mistake or a small one, we should ask for forgiveness and God will forgive us. It is also very important that, if we make a mistake we should ask for forgiveness from the person we have done wrong to. And, also, if someone by mistake does us wrong, and if they ask for forgiveness, we should forgive them because that is what God wants us to do.

Prayer: Let us pray, please repeat after me.
Dear God, thank you for loving us all the time. Thank you for this story. Please let us remember to ask for forgiveness when we do wrong. And help us to forgive those who need our forgiveness. In Jesus name we pray. Amen.

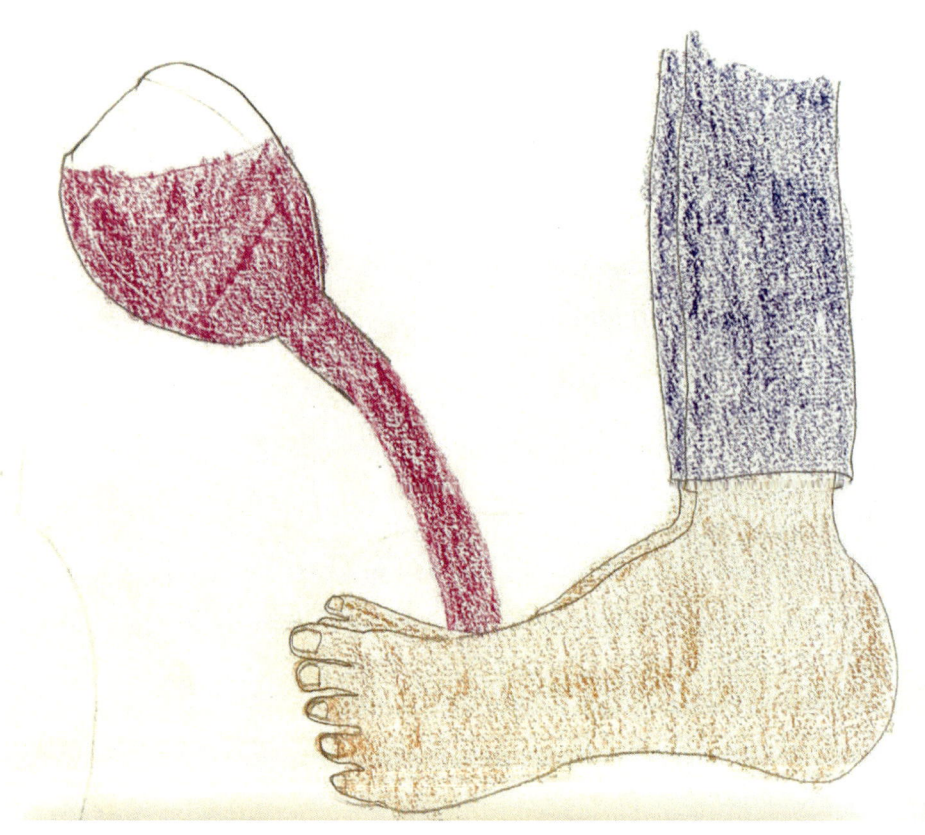

Fifth Sunday in Lent
April 3, 2022

John 12:1-8 Perfume on Jesus feet

Color Purple

Resource: a bottle of perfume

Children's Sermon: Have you ever smelled a nice perfume? *Let the Children answer you.*

Here it is. *Let the children smell a good perfume..*

We have been talking about God loving us. Jesus loving us and how and why we should love God, love one another and love neighbors.

In today's Bible lesson, we have a story of Mary washing Jesus' feet with a very good perfume and drying Jesus' feet with her hair. She wanted show Jesus her love and she did it that way. Jesus appreciated that very much.

Please don't take your mom's perfume and wash her feet though. She might not like that. Just tell her that you love her.

Prayer: Let us pray, please repeat after me.
Dear God, thank you for loving us all the time. Please teach us how to show you that we love you too. In Jesus name. Amen.

Palm Sunday - April 10, 2022

Luke 19:28-40 Jesus is our King
Color White

Resource: palm branches – enough for every child

Today is Palm Sunday!

Today we remember and celebrate Jesus as our King. Many years ago, Jesus went into the city called Jerusalem as a king, riding on a donkey no one had ever ridden. People were so happy that they put down their clothes on the ground for the donkey to walk on because it was carrying Jesus. They waved palm branches in their hands too just like you do now. *Let the children wave their palm branches.*

Let us walk to the front of the sanctuary waving the palms.

When I say: Blessed is he who comes in the name of the Lord,

you shout really loud saying, "Hosanna in the highest!!!"

That is what happened on that day in Jerusalem. Let's pretend that we are in Jerusalem and Jesus is coming to us riding on the new donkey. Ready? Let's go:

- You   "Blessed is he who comes in the name of the Lord!"
- Children   "Hosanna in the Highest!!!!"

Prayer: Let us pray, please repeat after me.
Dear God thank you for loving us all the time. Thank you for being our king. Hosanna in the highest. Amen.

Sunrise service, Siesta Key Beach, Sarasota, Florida

Easter Sunday
April 17

Luke 24:1-12; John 20:1-18 Jesus is risen!
Color White

Resource: a basket full of plastic eggs, bunnies, tulips and a picture of an empty cross

Childen's Sermon: Happy Easter! *Let the children respond to you.*

How wonderful is it that Jesus is risen from the dead and we celebrate Easter! Easter is not all about egg hunts, bunnies, flowers, peeps and cake. All those things are very good and enjoyable to celebrate the real reason. The real reason for Easter is that God loves us so much that God sent God's only son, Jesus, to live, die and be raised from the dead. Because of that, all of us are forgiven from our sins.

Where I grew up, we always say in my language, Mizo, "A tho ta! Isual Krista a tho ta!" that means "He is risen! Jesus Christ is risen!" How about I say " A tho ta!" and you all say back to me " Isua Krista a tho ta!". Ready:

- You   A tho ta!
- Children   Isua Krista a tho ta!

Prayer: Let us pray, please repeat after me.
Dear God, thank you for loving us all the time. Thank you for sending Jesus to us and raising him from the dead. Thank you also for our freedom to celebrate this Easter. We love you in Jesus name. Amen.

Second Sunday of Easter
April 24, 2022

John 20:19-31 Doubting Thomas
Color White

Resource: a picture of Thomas and Jesus

Children's Sermon: Have you ever doubted someone you love and you know loves you? *Let the children answer you.*

That happened to Thomas, one of Jesus' disciples. You know after Easter, when Jesus rose from the dead, he went to visit them in the room where most of his disciples were. Thomas was not there. So, his friends later told him that they saw Jesus. But Thomas did not believe them. He said, "Unless I see him in person and touch him myself, I will not believe that Jesus is alive."

A week later when all the disciples were together again, Jesus came and said to them, "Peace be with you."

Look at the children and say to them, can you say "Peace, be with you!"

Let the children say, "Peace be with you!" loudly.

And Jesus said to Thomas, "come touch my side and see that it is really me. Do not doubt but believe." Then Thomas said to Jesus, "my Lord and my God" and believed that it was Jesus.

Jesus said, "Blessed are those who believe without seeing me." That's us – that's you and me. We cannot see Jesus. We cannot see God or the Holy Spirit but we believe and know that God loves us always and God is always with us. We are the people Jesus called blessed.

Prayer: Let us pray, please repeat after me.
Dear God, thank you for loving us all the time. Thank you for helping us believe in your love and your presence even when we cannot see you. We love you in Jesus name. Amen.

Third Sunday of Easter
May 1, 2022

John 21:1-1 Breakfast with Jesus on the sea shore of the Sea of Tiberius
Color White

Resource: a picture of Jesus and the disciples on the shore eating

Children's Sermon: Have you ever had breakfast on the shore ever? *Let the children answer you.*

I have. Many times. When I was growing up, I spent every summer with my grandmother in her village. My grandmother loved to go fishing. We went fishing with three or four of her friends at least once a week. It was really fun. When we caught enough fish we stopped, cooked and ate the fish for a late breakfast or an early lunch. It was so tasty. They talked and laughed as they ate. I, as the only child in the group, listened and enjoyed being with them. It was a lot of fun. Even now as a 60 years old lady, I still go fishing with friends and enjoy it very much. And I eat the fish I catch too.

In today's scripture, we learned that Peter, Thomas, Nathaniel, James, John and 2 others were fishing all night and did not catch any fish. Jesus came to them and told them where to fish. They caught a lot of fish. When they came to the shore, they saw Jesus and fish cooking on the charcoal fire. Jesus invited them to come and eat with him. So, they went and had fish and bread for breakfast with Jesus. I love this story. Don't you? I hope so.

Prayer: Let us pray, please repeat after me.

Dear God, thank you for loving us all the time. Thank you for this wonderful story. Help us to find friends to do things with, even if it is not fishing. In Jesus name. Amen.

Fourth Sunday of Easter
May 8, 2022

John 10:22-30 Hearing Jesus' voice
Color White

Resource: a picture of someone calling someone else

Children's Sermon: When you are in the playground with your friends and your mom or dad come calling out your name what do you do? *Let the children answer you.* You say, "Hi mom/dad and ran to her/him and take the big hug from her or him. Right?" Why would you do that? *Let the children answer you.*

That's because you know that your parents love you and you love them.

In today's scripture lesson, Jesus said that those who love him know his voice because he loves them. That would be you and me. All of us. We know Jesus loves us. We will know when he calls us. Let us pray, please repeat after me.

Prayer:
Dear God, thank you for loving us all the time. Help us to love others like you love us. Help us to know your voice when you call us. In Jesus name. Amen.

Fifth Sunday of Easter
May 15, 2022

John 13:31-35 A Command to Love one another
Color White

Resources: pictures of people helping others and showing Christian love.

Children's Sermon: Today's scripture is one of my favorites, Jesus gave us a command. Jesus said to all of us, "I gave you a new commandment that you love one another. Just as I have loved you, you also should love one another. By this everyone will know that you are my followers."

Jesus loves us so very much. And he gave us a command to love one another. We can show that we love one another in many ways by:

- saying, "I love you,"
- helping others such as baby sitting a cat or a dog,
- talking to those who are lonely,
- playing with those who are shy and left out,
- being sweet to those who are old and lonely,
- being kind too everyone, and
- by speaking politely to all.

Prayer: Let us pray, please repeat after me.
Dear God, thank you for loving us all the time. We love you and we will love one another as Jesus commanded us. In Jesus' name. Amen.

VOICE OF LOVE!

Sixth Sunday of Easter
May 22, 2022

John 14:23-29 Jesus promised to send us Holy Spirit
Color White

Resources: A picture of Jesus talking to people. A picture of a Dove.

Children's Sermon: Sometimes moms and dads have to go somewhere for some important events such as dinner or a meeting or to the hospital to visit someone who is sick or for any good reason. They would say, "My dear, your favorite baby sitter will be here to watch over you. Don't forget to go to bed on time. Everything will be fine and we'll see you in the morning." You know you will be ok because your mom and dad told you so.

Very much like that Jesus told us in the Bible, just before he went home to God, that he will send the Holy Spirit to be with us. The Holy Spirit is like the air we breathe. It is always with us – loving us, comforting us, watching over us and praying for us. It is a very good thing. The Holy Spirit is here always. Let us pray, please repeat after me.

Prayer:
Dear God, thank you for loving us all the time. Teach us to know you more every day. Thank you for sending the Holy Spirit to be with us at all times. In Jesus' name Amen.

The Ascension Sunday
May 29, 2022

Luke 24:44-53 Jesus went home
Color White

Resource: a picture of Jesus going up to heaven

Children's Sermon:
Where do you go at the end of a play date, or school, or anywhere else you go? *Let the children answer you.*

Home, of course. But why would you go home? *Let the children answer you.*

We have been talking about Jesus making a promise to all of us that he would send the Holy Spirit after he returned home to God.

According to today's scripture, today we celebrate Jesus' return home to God. The actual anniversary of that day was last Thursday, the 26th. It is called "the Ascension Day." Jesus went home at the end of his work on earth.

Today is called the Ascension Sunday. Just as God sent Jesus to us at Christmas time, God also called Jesus to come home. So, Jesus went home to God in heaven. Let us pray, please repeat after me. *Let us pray, please repeat after me.*

Prayer:
Dear God, thank you for loving us all the time. Thank you for sending Jesus to us and taking him home to you again. We hope that somedday we will come home to you also. In Jesus name. Amen.

June. 5 2020

Pentecost Sunday Day
June 5, 2022

Acts 2:1-21 The Holy Spirit Came
Color Red

Resource: A red or orange paper cut out of a flame for each child.

Children's Sermon: This is Pentecost Sunday and we celebrate the Holy Spirit coming down from heaven. Many years ago people from all over the world came together to Jerusalem to celebrate the Jewish Pentecost Day. They were from literally from all over the world including from Asia and Egypt. Everyone had his or her own culture and language. When they were together the Holy Spirit came down from heaven like the rush of a violent wind. It filled the entire place.

Give the microphone to a child or two and ask them to blow into it to demonstrate the " violent rush of wind."

It was much stronger and louder than that sound. Pretty impressive. *Yeah? Let the children talk.*

Bible tells us that the Holy Spirit came above each of them like a candle flame and they came to understand each other – just like that. The same holy spirit is given to us, all of us now. Yes, you too. God has given you the Holy Spirt to be with you always. Take a flame with you to remind you of that. Let us pray. Please repeat after me.

Prayer:
Dear God, thank you for loving us all the time. Thank you for sending us the holy spirit. We love you. In Jesus' name.

God
The
Father

Holy Spirit
The
Sustainer

Jesus The Son

Trinity Sunday
June 12, 2022

John 16:12-15 Three in one
Color White

Resource: Have a sheet of paper for every child with a drawing of a Triangle on it.

- On one corner write God the Father.
- On the second on corner write Jesus the Son.
- On the last corner write Holy Spirit the Sustainer.

As the children come up give each child a sheet of this paper and invite them to sit down before you talk to them.

Children's Sermon: Hello everyone, please look at the paper I handed you. What do you see? *Let the children answer you.*

Would someone like to read the writing on the paper? *Let a child read it to the group.*

That's right. We believe in a God who is three in one. God is the Father and Jesus is the Son and the Holy Spirit is the sustainer. God is always with us even when we are not thinking about it..

Remember last Sunday, we talked about how the holy spirit came down from God and fell on each and every one on Pentecost Day a long long time ago in Jerusalem. Tthe holy spirit is on every one of us today too. Holy spirit is like a good mother to us. Our God is called a Triune God. Let us pray. Repeat after me, please.

Prayer:
Dear God, thank you for loving us all the time. Thank you for being our God who is always with us. Teach us to understand you as Father, Son and Holy Spirit. In Jesus name. Amen.

Chains

*BRO**K***EN****

Second Sunday after Pentecost
June 19, 2022

Luke 8:26-39 Unbinding the strongman
Color Green

Resource: a big and strong chain

Children's Sermon: A long time ago, there was a man who lived in a town near where Jesus lived. The man had a lot of evil in him. He was very strong. The people were afraid of him. They tried to tie him up with chains but he broke the chains.

One day Jesus came and saw him and Jesus freed the man from the evil. Jesus knew God loves this man because God loves everyone. This man went from scaring people to telling people how good God is.

We can be scary to others if we are mean and unkind to them. But, if we remember how much God loves us, we may be less angry and more friendly. I suggest that we stay loving God and being kind to others. Let us pray. Please repeat after me.

Prayer:
Dear God, thank you for loving us all the time. Thank you for Jesus and his power. Teach us to be kind and thankful like this man in today's Bible story. In Jesus' name. Amen.

Day and night,

God

loves

us!

Third Sunday after Pentecost
June 26, 2022

Psalm 16 Keeping God before me always
Color Green

Resource: a picture of a child following a parent

Children's Sermon: One of my favorite Psalms is Psalm 16. It reminds me to put God first, before myself, always. What that means is that I follow God like you follow your mom and dad. You do that because you know they love you and they want what's best for you. God is like that for all of us. God knows what is best for us. God wants what's best for us. Because God really loves us. Let us pray. Please repeat after me.

Prayer:
Dear God, thank you for loving us all the time. Thank you for our moms and dads who love us. Teach us to how to follow you every day. In Jesus name. Amen.

WE THANK GOD
FOR OUR FREEDOM!

Fourth Sunday after Pentecost
July 3, 2022

Psalm 30:4 Freedom
Color Green

Resources: One large American Flag and small ones to give to the children

Look at this big flag, why do you think I brought this to show it to you.

Let the children answer you.

Yes, tomorrow is the 4th of July as we know it! It is a day to celebrate our independence as a nation. Here, have a flag – each of you. Tomorrow we will remember how God is blessing us every day of our lives. We will remember those who fought for our freedom and independence. We are free in this country to speak our minds, to live without fear and to worship God without any problem. We are so blessed. Of course, we will also eat lots of good food with family and friends to celebrate.

The scripture today tells us to sing praises to God and give thanks to God. So, please wave your flags as you repeat after me. Let us pray:

Prayer:
Dear God, thank you for loving us all the time. We thank you and praise you for giving us freedom to speak and worship you in this nation. In Jesus' name. Amen.

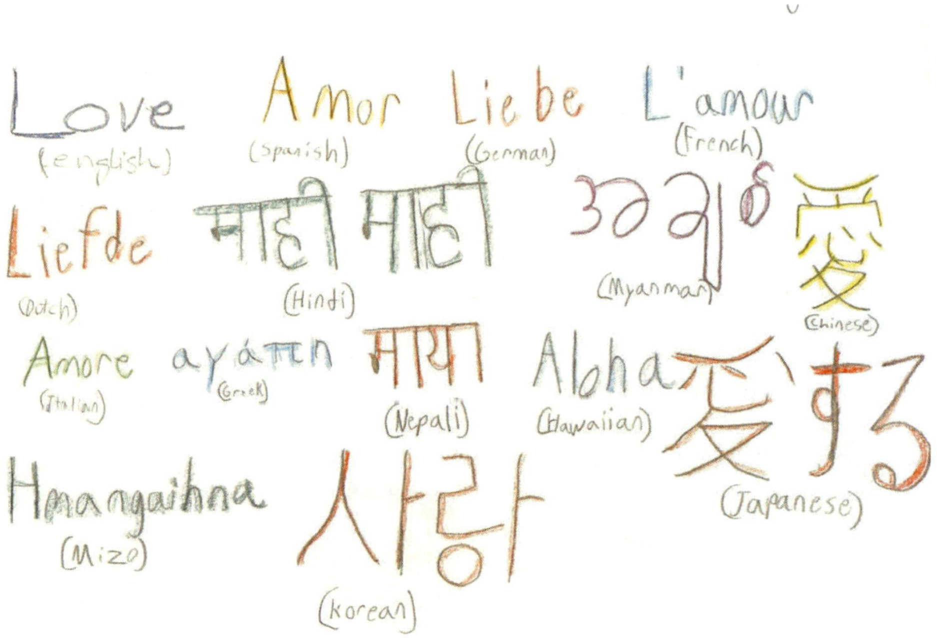

Love
(english)

Amor
(spanish)

Liebe
(German)

L'amour
(French)

Liefde
(Dutch)

माही माही
(Hindi)

အချစ်
(Myanmar)

愛
(Chinese)

Amore
(Italian)

αγάπη
(Greek)

माया
(Nepali)

Aloha
(Hawaiian)

愛する
(Japanese)

Hmangaihna
(Mizo)

사랑
(Korean)

Fifth Sunday after Pentecost
July 10, 2022

Luke 10:25-37 Love God, self and neighbor
Color Green

Resources: Construction paper. On each piece of paper, the word "Love" is written in a different language such as, English, Spanish, Chinese, Hindi, German, French. Have as many languages as you like.

Children's Sermon How do you say love in English? *Let the children answer you.*

They may giggle and say, "Love"

Show one of the construction papers that says Love in "Spanish."

Ask the children, "What does this say?" *Let the children answer you. You tell them. Do the same for each construction paper of the word love in different languages.*

Jesus said love God, and love your neighbor as yourself. So, who are our neighbors? All the people who speak all these languages and more are our neighbors. Let us pray, please repeat after me.

Prayer:
Dear God, thank you for loving us all the time. Thank you for giving us all our neighbors. Teach us how to love them. In Jesus' name. Amen.

Listening

Or

Serving

-

Which is Most Important?

Sixth Sunday after Pentecost
July 17, 2022

Luke 10:38-42 Mary and Martha story
Color Green

Resources: A Bible, pots and pans and plates.

Children's Sermon: Do you have a brother or a sister? *Let the children answer you.*

What do your brothers or sisters do? Do they clean up the room? Help in the kitchen? Or do you do that? *Let the children answer you.*

In our scripture today there are two sisters – Mary and Martha. They are both friends of Jesus. One day Jesus came to visit them. Martha went into the kitchen right away to make food and drinks for Jesus. Mary just sat with Jesus in the living room and listened to Jesus' talk. Martha thought Mary should help her in the kitchen. But. really, they both need to do both things, I think. When the time comes to eat, Mary and Jesus will be hungry and there will be no food. So, actually both Martha and Mary were right. Except that they should both cook and they should both listen to Jesus. What do you think? *Let the children answer you.*

My sister-in-law used to say, many different things can be true at the same time. Joan was right. Mary and Martha both were right with their own points at the same time.

Let us pray, please repeat after me.

Prayer:
Dear God, thank you for loving us all the time. Please teach us to know when to listen to you and when to get busy doing what needs to be done. In Jesus' name. Amen.

Our Father, who art in heaven
Hallowed by thy name.
Thy kingdom come, thy will be done,
On earth as it is in Heaven.
Give us this day our daily bread
And forgive our debts,
as we forgive our debtors.
Lead us not into temptation
But deliver us from evil.
For thine is the kingdom, the power
And the glory, for ever and ever. Amen.

Seventh Sunday after Pentecost
July 24, 2022

Luke 11:1-13 The Lord's Prayer
Color Green

Resources: a picture of Jesus teaching the disciples

Children's Sermon: The disciples of Jesus did not know how to pray and they asked Jesus to teach them how to pray. So, Jesus taught his disciples how to pray. The prayer is like this.
Please close your eyes and repeat after me.

"Our Father, who is in heaven, holy be your name.
Your kingdom come.
Give us each day our daily bread;
and forgive us our sins as we forgive those who sin against us.
And, do not bring us to the time of trial."

In Jesus' name we pray. Amen. This prayer got expanded to be a bit longer as time went on and we now call it "The Lord's Prayer." That's the children's sermon for today.

Eighth Sunday after Pentecost
July 31, 2022

Luke 12:13-23 What to do if you are rich?
Color Green

Resources: In a bag put a pair of sneakers, three pairs of sandals, and a pair of hi heels. If you are a man, please put equivalent items in the bag.

Children's Sermon: Do you want lots of money? *Let the children answer you.*

I know it is a big question.

What would you do with your money if you have a lot of it. *Let the children answer you.*

If we have a lot of money, we can buy lots of things that we need and some things we don't need but want.

Look, here. I have a pair of walking shoes I need. I have three pairs of sandals that I need. Not really, I only need one pair. I should donate the other two pairs. Right? And this, dress shoes on my feet (point at tmy shoes for the children to see.) I have three more pairs at home. do I need them all? Yes! I do need them all. I have to come to work every day in them. And look in my hands. A pair of high heels that I love. Do I need them? I have it because I love it.

The scripture lesson today tells us that there is a rich man who thought he was going to live forever and stored up all his wealth. But, Jesus said to him that he should share his riches and be happy sharing. The message is the same to us today. We should be generous and share with others. Let us pray, please repeat after me.

Prayer:
Dear God, thank you for loving us all the time. Help us to remember to be generous and share what we have with others. In Jesus' name we pray. Amen.

74

Ninth Sunday after Pentecost
August 7, 2022

Luke 12:32-40 Where your treasure is, there your hearts will be also.
Color Green

Resource: Have a treasure box with your family picture, and a few more items that you treasure.

Children's Sermon: Do you know what this box is? *Let the children answer you.*

Yes, it is my treasure box. Does anyone else have a treasure box? *Let the children answer you. If anyone said yes, ask, "Please tell me what's in your treasure box?" Let the children answer you.*

Just like you I have some things that are so very important to me that I keep them safe in this box. In my treasure box are…. *Show them one item at a time and tell them why it is a treasure to you.*

Jesus said, in our scripture today, "where your treasure is, there your heart will be also." Our best treasure is not what is in our boxes but it is in God's love for us. God loves us always no matter what. That is the best treasure we have. Would you please remember that? And, it is perfectly alright to have a treasure box too. Let us pray. please repeat after me.,

Prayer:
Dear God, thank you for loving us all the time. Thank you for making your love our treasure. Help us to always remember that you are the best treasure we have. In Jesus' name. Amen.

Tenth Sunday after Pentecost
August 14, 2022

Psalm 80:1-3 Caring with love.
Color Green

Resource: A picture of your pet and family or other pictures.

My granddaughters, Lilly and Emmy, have a dog named Daphne. They got Daphne when she was only 6 weeks old. They love her so very much. Daphne loves them too. They made her a very comfortable bed. They made sure she ate every meal and was healthy. They walked her every day. They protected Daphne from all the big dogs and anything that might harm her. When my husband and I visited them, it was really fun to watch how my young granddaughters age 5 and 9 were so protective and caring of their pet dog, Daphne.

Do you have a pet? Are you like my granddaughters? *Let the children answer you.*

Keep loving your pat and take care of him or her. I don't have a pet but my husband is like my pet. I love him and take very good care of him. He loves me and takes good care of me too.

The Scripture tells us that God is like that for us always. God blesses us and loves us and makes sure we are ok. God protects us and provides all our needs. Let us pray, please repeat after me.

Prayer:
Dear God, thank you for loving us all the time. Thank you for watching over us and giving us all our needs. Help us to love those who are near us including our pets. In Jesus' name. Amen.

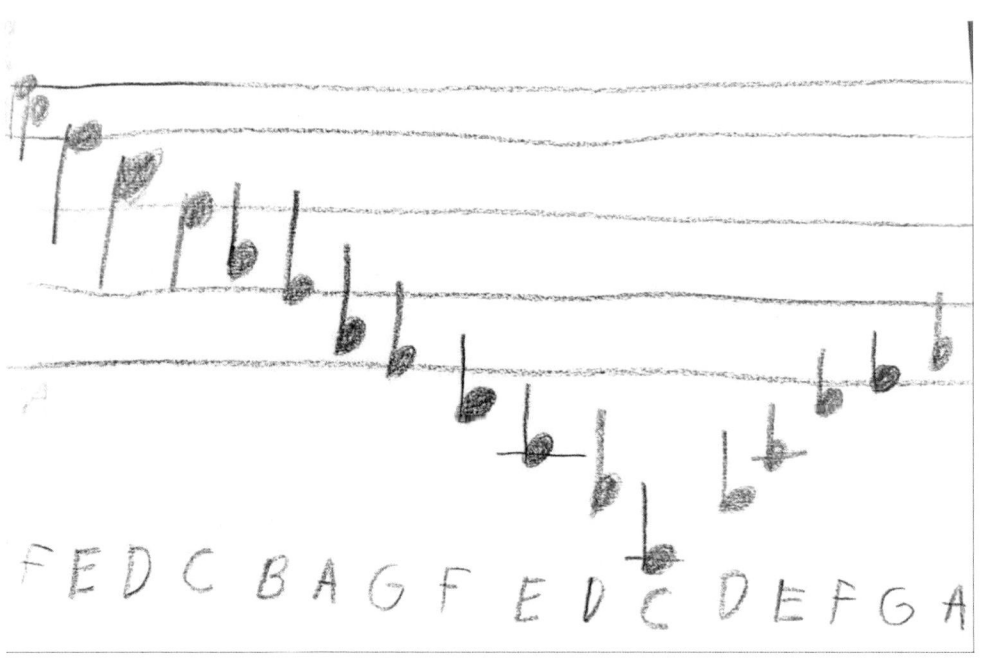

Eleventh Sunday after Pentecost
August 21, 2022

Psalm 71:1-6 Why praise God?
Color Green

Resource: toy musical instruments of different kinds in a bag

Children's Sermon: Pull out an instrument and ask the children, "What is this?" *Let the children answer you.*

Do the same with all the rest of the instrument's and let the children give you their comments.

"What are these instruments for?" *Let the children answer you.*

"Yes, these instruments are used to make music. Most of the time, music makes us happy and we make music because we are happy." In the Church, we use musical instruments to praise God and to say "thank you" to God.

The Psalmist says to us in today's scripture that he praises God all the time because of God's goodness to him and his hope in God. I suggest that next time you hear music or when you play music you all remember how good God is to you. Let us pray, please repeat after me.

Prayer:
Dear God, thank you for loving us all the time. Please help us to remember to praise you for your goodness and love for us. In Jesus' name. Amen.

WE CAN

ALWAYS

HELP

OTHERS.

Twelfth Sunday after Pentecost
August 28, 2022

Luke 14:1, 7-14 Be humble and kind to the poor
Color Green

Resource: A picture of a leper and his son or something similar.

Children's Sermon: When I was growing up in Myanmar my parents were doing pretty well. There was a beggar with his son, a 3 years old boy. He was the cutest and sweetest little boy. The father had a skin sickness called leprosy. The boy had no mother. They walked by our house every morning and every evening. In the morning my mother would say hello to them and give them breakfast to eat. The little boy would play with my younger brother and sisters on the weekends and in the evenings. In the evenings my mom would give them dinner. The father would never come into our house, so they ate at our front porch and we would go out and eat with them sometimes. But we would always play with the little boy. We did not know where they lived as the man would not tell us. We just saw them in the mornings and in the evenings and on the weekends.

My mom would give the little boy some clothes of my brother's to wear.
I remember them even now. It was so good to be there for them. We did not know where they were. One day, they stopped walking by our house and we never saw them again. My mom did not do any of the kindness to this man and his son because she wanted anything back from them. My mom did all that she did for them because she loved God and she knew God loved this man and his son.

Jesus tells us that we should do good for the poor not because we want something in return but because God loves them as much as God loves us. And because we love God. Let us pray, please repeat after me.

Prayer:
Dear God, thank you for loving us all the time. Thank you for loving all the people. Teach us to show your love to others including to the poor. In Jesus' name. Amen.

God

knows us

inside

and

out!

Thirteenth Sunday after Pentecost
September 4, 2022

Psalm 139:1-6 God knows us completely
Color Green

Resource: A picture of a fetus, a picture of a baby and a toddler, a group picture of children of all ages, a group picture of mixed generations of adults and a picture of old people. Or, one picture of people of all generations.

Children's Sermon: What kind of people do you see in this picture? *Let the children answer you.*

Do you see people of your age? *Let the children answer you.*

I hope so. Can you believe that God knows you and me and all the people even before we are born? *Let the children make comments.*

Yes, God does know us. God created us. God knows us very very well all the time from before we were born until we die God sees us and loves us every moment of every day. How do I know that? Because the Bible tells me so. Let us pray, please repeat after me.

Prayer:
Dear God, thank you for loving us all the time. Thank you for creating us. Please help us to be good people. In Jesus' name. Amen.

Fourteenth Sunday after Pentecost
September 11, 2022

Luke 15:1-10 Lost sheep
Color Green

Resource: A toy stuffed sheep, a toy man and other toy people.

Children's Sermon: In the Bible lesson to day, there was a guy who lost his sheep and he went looking for it and finally found it. He was so happy that he found his lost sheep. He brought the sheep home and went out and invited his neighbors to celebrate the finding of his sheep. They did. I bet there was food and juice and happy talk and laughing among them.

God loves us all and even when we feel bad and we misbehave God still loves us. God celebrates us when we return to God. Let us pray, please repeat after me.

Prayer:
Dear God, thank you for loving us all the time. Help us to stay with you and not to wonder away from your love. In Jesus' name. Amen.

Fifteenth Sunday after Pentecost
September 18, 2022

Luke 16:1-13 The importance of honesty
Color Green

Resource: an empty bowl and a raw egg

I need a volunteer to hold the bowl please. *Give the bowl to the volunteer and crack the egg and pour the content into the bowl. Ask the children if that can be put back together again. Let them answer you.*

Our words and our actions are very much like the egg you just saw. Once we say or do something, it is really impossible to repair it. The Bible tells us to be faithful and truthful and honest with our words and actions every day. We should do our best to do that. We will still make mistakes, but it is best that we try to live an honest life.

Let us pray, please repeat after me.

Prayer:
Dear God, thank you for loving us all the time. Thank you for giving us good brains and hearts to think and feel. Help us to use them to be honest and truthful and faithful to you and to others. In Jesus' name. Amen.

Sixteenth Sunday after Pentecost
September 25, 2022

Psalm 91:1-6; 14-16 God as a protecting Eagle
Color Green

Resource: a large size toy eagle and small size toy people

Children's Sermon: See these toy people under the wings of the eagle. I can fit all the toy people there. Just imagine yourselves to be a part of these toy people. Would you feel safe and happy there? *Let the children answer you.*

The Bible tells us that God is like a very big and loving and powerful Eagle, big enough that the whole world can be under God's wings. God loves each and every one of us and God is always protecting us and making sure we are alright. Don't you think that's really good? *Let the children answer you.*

Let us pray, please repeat after me.

Prayer:
Dear God, Thank you for loving us all the time. Thank you for protecting us and making us safe. Teach us to be thankful to you. We love you. In Jesus' name. Amen.

Seventieth Sunday after Pentecost/World Communion Sunday
October 2

Luke 17:5-10 the whole world feasts at the same table
Color White

Resources: A basket of breads from different culture such as Nan, Lavash, sourdough, rice cake etc. And a bottle of grape juice.

Children's Sermon: Today is one of my favorite Sundays. It is called World Communion Sunday. That means all the Christian people around the world are having communion today. Jesus said whenever you eat this bread, remember me. So, people around the world are having different kinds of bread and remembering Jesus and God's love. The same way, Jesus said, "every time you drink this remember me." The most important thing to me is that all of us who have faith in God and believe in Jesus are having the same meal today.

Only once a year, on the first Sunday of October, we do this. Please remember that every time you take communion, you are saying to God, "Thank you God for loving me and I love you too." Let us pray, please repeat after me.

Prayer:
Dear God, Thank you for loving us all the time. Help us to remember how much you love us every time we take communion. In Jesus' name. Amen.

Eighteenth Sunday after Pentecost
October 9, 2022

Psalm 66:1-12 Make a joyful noise
Color Green

Resources: In a bag bring different musical instruments you don't mind the children using.

Children's Sermon: Give an *instrument to each child and have them all make sound of what they each are holding. If you have a big crowd of them ask for volunteers for the numbers of the musical instruments you have. You hold one instrument yourself and say,* "Jesus loves us and we are happy about it. Right?" *Let the children answer you.*

Now at my count of three those who have an instrument make noise with it. Those of you who don't have an instrument please sing loudly whatever is your favorite Christian song - like, "Jesus loves me." Ready, one two, three. Go!

Lots of noises and voices. And lots of smiles and giggles.

The Bible tells us to make a joyful noise to the Lord. We just did that. God does not expect us to have a perfect singing voice or perfect musical skill. God will take any happy and joyful noise we give God. Because God loves us no matter what. Let us pray, repeat after me please.

Prayer:
Dear God, thank you for loving us all the time. Boy - that was fun to make a joyful noise to you. Help us to remember to make a joyful noise to you more often. We love you. In Jesus' name. Amen.

I lift up my eyes

to the hills –

From where will

my help

come?

My help comes

from the LORD,

who made

heaven and earth...

Nineteenth Sunday after Pentecost
October 16, 2022

Psalm 121 Ask God for help
Color Green

Resources: A picture of a child praying, and a picture of Jesus with children.

Children's Sermon: I am not sure if I ever told you that I love the Psalms in the Bible. They are like poetry. There are 150 of them in the Bible. I read some of them every day first thing in the morning. The Psalm for today is Psalm 121. It tells us that we should ask God to help us when we get into trouble of any kind. That means we talk to God which is also called praying.

When I was about 5 years old, I broke my mom's favorite flower vase. Boy, did I know that I was in trouble. I went to a corner and said to God, "Dear God, I am so sorry that I broke my mom's favorite flower vase. Please let her not be mad at me. I know she will be sad but please let her believe that I did not mean to break it. In Jesus' name. Amen."

Then I took the broken vase to my mom. I was so scared. I told my mom that I was very sorry that I broke her favorite vase and it was an accident. Guess what? *Let the children answer you.*

Mom said, "Breakables do get broken some times. I am glad you came to tell me the truth." She gave me a hug. I cried because I could tell my mom loved me very much.

The Bible tells us in Psalm 121 that we should go to God and talk to God whenever we are in trouble. It could be being sick, an accident, or breaking stuff like I did or having told a lie, among many other things. The most important thing is that we talk to God. Let us pray, please repeat after me.

Prayer:
Dear God, thank you for loving us all the time. You know we get in trouble sometimes. Please help us to come to you with all our troubles small and big. In Jesus' name. Amen.

Twentieth Sunday after Pentecost
October 23, 2022

Psalm 84:1-7 the beauty of heaven
Color Green

Resources: Some flowers, some pictures of springs, birds and other pleasant things

Children's Sermon: How do you feel when you see flowers and pictures like these?

Let the children answer you.

Do you ever draw or paint or pick flowers? Or do you ever see pretty birds?

Let the children answer you.

Well, the scripture today tells us that God's house in heaven is full of beautiful and pretty things like these and more. It is a beautiful place. Someday, we'll all get to be there in person. Let us pray, please repeat after me.

Prayer:
Dear God, thank you for loving us all the time. Thank you for the picture of your house we get to imagine - up there in the heavens. We love you God. In Jesus' name. Amen.

All Saints Sunday/Twenty-first Sunday after Pentecost

October 30, 2022

Luke 19:1-10 Almost Halloween…

Color White

Resources: A plastic pumpkin trick or treat container and candies inside.

Children's Sermon: Tomorrow is a special day. Does anyone know why? And what is it called? *Let the children answer you.*

Yes, it is Halloween! It is my favorite holiday because people are friendlier. The open their front doors to the trick or treaters. The first year I was in this country as an international student, I was surprised that people don't visit each other in their homes. I mean they don't just drop in and knock on the door to visit. They had to call and make an appointment for a visit.

Then came the Halloween evening, most everyone opened their door to the little people and not so little people in costumes and baskets. They opened their door even to those they did not know personally. I was so happy to see that. It became my favorite holiday because people are friendly that day. They even smile to the trick or treaters and give them candies.

Halloween means, "All Hallow's Eve" which means the day before "All Saint's Day" - which is always November 1st. All Saints Day is a day to remember all the saints - all the people we love who have gone home to God.

Today is called All Saints Sunday as we will not be in church on November 1st. We thank God for all the saints in the Church today. We remember them and celebrate their lives and we say thank you to God for them. Would you please remember all the saints tomorrow when you go trick or treating? A part of our scripture today tells us that Salvation has come to Zacchaeus' house as he was a saint. If you cannot remember many saints tomorrow, please remember to say to God, "Thank you God for a saint named Zacchaeus." Let us pray, please repeat after me.

Prayer:

Dear God, thank you for loving us all the time. Thank you for all the saints we know and the saints we don't know because you know them all. Tomorrow on Halloween, please keep us safe and help us remember a saint or two as we have fun 'trick or treating.' In Jesus' name. Amen.

Twenty Second Sunday after Pentecost
November 6, 2022

Psalm 134:17-21 God is always near.
Color Green

Resource: A Bible

Children's Sermon: When I was little I used to have nightmares in my sleep. I would cry out or I would scream or I would make some noise. My dad came right over to my bed. He would say, "Mami (that's my nick name), you are having a bad dream. Would you like to wake up and tell me about it?" I would tell him my dream sometimes. Most of the time he would rub my back and I would fall back to sleep with him sitting on my bed. It did not matter if I had one bad dream or more, my dad would be right there. I really loved that. I knew I didn't have to be afraid of bad dreams even in the darkness of the night.

The scriptures today tell us that God is always near to those who call on him. If we call God is here. God is watching over all of us who love him. When I think of God being near me, I know it is real just like my dad was real to me. Let us pray, please repeat after me.

Prayer:
Dear God, thank you for loving us all the time. Please help us to know to call on you when we need you. Thank you for being near to us all the time. In Jesus' name. Amen.

Twenty Third Sunday after Pentecost
November 13, 2022

Psalm 98 Singing a new song
Color Green

Resource: A music sheet of a simple new song the children don't know

Children's Sermon: Can you sing a new song? *Let the children answer you.*

I was born and I grew up in a country named Myanmar. We had many happy songs to praise God as children that I learned and loved singing. Can one of you sing a song you know to us now.

Let a volunteer or two sing.

When I got older, I went to study in other countries - in India and Korea. There I learned to sing many new songs in English to praise God.

All of us keep learning to sing a new songs as we grow. Just remember that God likes that very much. Sing to God a new song even in English. God likes that. How do I know that? Because the Bible tells me so. Let us pray, please repeat after me.

Prayer:
Dear God, thank you for loving us all the time. Please teach us to sing a new song to praise you. In Jesus' name. Amen.

Christ the King/Thanksgiving Sunday
November 20, 2022

Psalm 118:1-4; 24-29 Giving Thanks
Color White

Resource: A cornucopia full of plastic or real vegetables and fruits.

Children's Sermon: Do you know what this thing I brought to show you is? What is it?

Let the children answer you.

In a few days we are going to celebrate Thanksgiving Day. It is a wonderful day to eat a lot, to be with family and friends, to invite those who are lonely and have nowhere to go. Most of all it is a day to give thanks to God big time for all God's blessings to us every day.

The scripture tells us to give thanks to the lord because God is good to us and God loves us always. Let us pray, please repeat after me.

Prayer:
Dear God, thank you for loving us all the time. Thank you for all your blessings we receive every day. Help us to invite and include other people on Thanksgiving Day. In Jesus name. Amen.